MW00588267

Navigating Your Fertility as a Woman in Medicine

Jenna Miller, MD

Navigating Your Fertility as a Woman in Medicine
©2023, Jenna Miller, MD

ISBN: 978-1-66789-621-2
ISBN eBook: 978-1-66789-622-9

Dedication

This book is dedicated to all the people who supported me on this journey—my family, friends, and coworkers. Everyone deserves a village like you. A special thank you to my mom for sitting with me through all the many procedures and then reading this guide multiple times to help with its delivery!

Preface

This book is for anyone in the profession of medicine who wishes to think about or plan for a family. While the content is from the perspective of a female physician, the content and tips can be applied across medicine and to any profession with delayed timelines for family planning and/or atypical work schedules. Those who may find it useful include women, men supporting women, same-sex couples, LGBTQIA+ individuals, and others who may need assistance in starting a family.

My fertility journey began when I was thirty-five. At the age of forty-two, it is not over, and I have learned a great deal about approaches to building a family. During this time, I have tried to help younger physicians learn about their own fertility and make educated choices concerning family planning. I describe my journey in this guide and share information for navigating family planning as a member of the medical profession. I have experienced many nontraditional routes to family planning, including adoption, in vitro fertilization, and gestational carriers. The information in this guide is based on my personal experience and learning. There is evidence-based information current as of 2022 when this book was written that is referenced in the following chapters. The combination of my experiences in assisted reproductive technology and medical literature is summarized in this guide to raise awareness of the issues one may face when confronting fertility issues. There are numerous approaches to this journey, and there are many ways people will experience those approaches. Finances also vary across geographic portions of the United States, and this was my experience in the Midwest. So, this is not a "one-size-fits-all" description of the journey; however, the issues raised can be generalized to many.

I truly hope it can help others.

Disclaimer

I am not a reproductive endocrinologist. All medical decision making should be between you and your personal physician; this guide does not take the place of professional medical advice.

Table of Contents

I

The Truth About Infertility

Infertility is defined as the inability to conceive after one year of unprotected sex, but the time span is sometimes decreased to six months if an individual is older than thirty-five.[1] The use of assisted reproductive technology (ART) is aimed at treating infertility and has doubled in use in the past decade now accounting for 2 percent of all live births in the United States.[2] There are over 8 million people who have been born via ART since the first ART birth in 1978.[3] As of 2020, over 300,000 ART procedures are performed annually in over 400 clinics in the United States, leading to approximately 75,000 to 80,000 annual births.[2]

According to the Center for Disease Control (CDC), 19 percent of the general United States population experiences infertility, which was previously reported at 12 percent until 2021.[1] In 2016, 24 percent of women working as physicians reported infertility, but it is possible this number has increased along with national trends reported by the CDC.[4] In 2017, 29 percent of medical resident physicians reported infertility, while nearly two-thirds reported feeling little support from their training programs.[5] A career in medicine often leads to starting family planning later than women in the general population,[6,7] and while not all factors are understood, female physicians have higher rates of infertility when they do attempt to start families.[7] Along with higher infertility rates for physicians, there are also higher pregnancy complication rates, including a doubled miscarriage rate.[7]

Reports in 2021 and 2022 by the American Association of Medical Colleges indicate that there are over 96,000 medical students in training, and over 51,000 of them identify as women.[8] There are over 149,000 residents and fellows in training, and 70,500 are women, an increase of 6,400 since the 2020 data was released.[9] There are also around 120,000 practicing female physicians under the age of forty.[10] Therefore, there is nearing 250,000 women physician trainees or early career physicians, and a portion of these may be in a position to need family planning support. This figure does not include men supporting women partners, LGBTQIA+ individuals, or individuals in same-sex relationships who may also need this information.

In this guide, I share my own story of infertility while being a woman in medicine. I personally did not realize the high probability that my fertility would be so impacted by my mid-thirties. Like many trainees, I took a conventional route through medical school, residency, and fellowship. I did not complete my pediatric critical care training until I was thirty-two years old, and I did not consider fertility preservation at that time. I had always wanted and expected to be a mother, and so, at the age of thirty-five, I sought the expertise of a reproductive endocrinologist to better understand my options. I learned quickly that my ovarian reserve, an indicator of women's fertility, was already severely diminished. I was originally counseled not to pursue egg cryopreservation (freezing), and I followed that advice at the time as my chance for a live birth was estimated to be around 30 percent. This is the first time I remember feeling sadness and experiencing grief in what would end up being a long journey in the infertility process. I went to a David Bowie cover band concert that night and tried to forget the overwhelming and disheartening news. Reflecting on my journey, my first regret is that I waited to investigate and understand my own fertility, and my second regret is that I did not pursue egg freezing after my original consultation. Even though my chances were low for any given retrieval, I eventually went through four retrievals, and having done those earlier may have changed my outcome. I often reflect that since I am in medicine, perhaps there was an assumption I knew what to do next in difficult circumstances. I wish I would have asked my reproductive endocrinologists more questions and inquired, "What would you do next?" more often.

Many of my friends, colleagues, and trainees have also experienced disappointment in this process; thus, I know I am not alone and some of my story is not unique. I have, however, experienced a large variety of procedures over the past seven years and understand the options available to those of us who choose or need to pursue nontraditional pathways to building a family, as well as some of the emotional and/or physical hardships associated with those pathways. I also experienced this journey as a single woman and found myself in the company of a fierce group of women who identify as Single Moms by Choice or Choice Moms. In the following chapters, I discuss nontraditional options for those who are considering starting or continuing a family. There is a lot of information, and you may decide to focus on those chapters that pertain to your unique fertility journey. Since I am quite a task-oriented planner, I developed some easy "To-Do" lists for each stage, which you can find at the end of this guide. To anyone reading these chapters, I wish you success in your endeavors. If so inclined, share your stories with me on Twitter @JennaMillerKC or connect with me via my website, jennamillermd.com.

2

Infertility Education for Medical Trainees

Despite the frequency of infertility experienced by medical professionals and families, infertility planning is not commonly discussed during medical training. This culture is perhaps in the early stages of changing, which is essential for those who wish to plan for or pursue a family. However, it is past time to change the paucity of discussion and focus on supporting the reproductive health of our medical professionals. Normalizing the conversation around fertility so that students, trainees, and early-career physicians can speak freely about infertility is imperative. I hope that current and future professionals in medicine will be informed as to how common infertility is in general and how our profession can prepare one to face challenges in family planning. I wish this information had been made available during my medical training. I believe my life would likely look very different now had I pursued fertility options when I was younger.

There are over 245,000 people training in medical school and residency right now in the United States and over 121,000 of them identify as women.[8,9] It is our collective job to ensure the current and future generations of training physicians understand how to preserve their fertility at the right time.

To accomplish this goal, I think there are three broad and important goals to address in the education of training physicians. They are:

1. Include fertility curricula in medical schools, residencies, and fellowship programs that incorporate information on age-related changes to fertility and the medical treatment available to them.

2. Increase the transparency of fertility preservation resources available in the community and within their insurance plan.

3. Allow for an open dialogue on what is necessary to accommodate individuals pursuing fertility treatments–including, but not limited to, time off and scheduling changes.

With the current lack of consistency in curricula delivered around this topic, we must empower ourselves to independently address the topic.

As a pediatric critical care fellowship program director, I began encouraging transparency in conversation by discussing fertility information with my trainees. I incorporated fertility information into annual orientation, outlined leave expectations in our orientation manual, and introduced fertility as a retreat topic. I encouraged individualized discussions, where one could explore if they wanted to evaluate their fertility with their personal physicians.

One of my previous trainees, who pursued ART during training, shared the following statement and consented to be identified:

"I strongly believe that I would not have been able to accomplish the number of intrauterine insemination (IUI) and *in vitro* fertilization (IVF) cycles that I did during fellowship if not for my program director having lived through the infertility treatments herself and being supportive and understanding."
—Aliza Olive, MD, Pediatric Critical Care Physician

My hope is that a trainee will be supported to pursue the treatments necessary for them, even if their program director doesn't have the knowledge or extensive experience in ART that I have. There are basic steps as outlined previously that programs can take to make their institutions supportive of all forms of family planning.

Within our current culture, we have neither made this type of support common nor mandated fertility curriculums in training programs as part of whole physician wellness. Perhaps, one day, fertility training for medical trainees will be included, and the policy changes needed to allow fertility pursuit for trainees and early-career physicians will follow. This happens only when an issue becomes more commonly understood and openly discussed.

3

Thinking About Fertility at the Right Time

I recall knowing at an early age that I wanted to be a parent. Several years ago, I found a time capsule I had made in second grade. The time capsule contained sketches and timelines of how I saw my life unfolding. Very prominently, I had foreseen becoming a mother in my twenties. Yet when I found this time capsule, I was in my mid-thirties, and it struck me that even in my early thirties, I would not have predicted my progression on an infertility path. One does not think infertility is going to happen to them, and society has conditioned us to believe everyone can travel the same pathway to family building. However, female fertility begins to decline at age thirty with a more rapid decline by the mid-thirties.[11] Available egg reserves, also referred to as ovarian reserves, decrease over time, as do the chances of successful pregnancies. At the same time, the risk of chromosome abnormalities increases.[12]

As the average age of first birth in the United States has risen from just over twenty-one years to just shy of twenty-seven years, it should not come as a surprise that more women find themselves struggling with infertility.[13] My fertility preservation story doesn't begin until my mid-thirties, and for me, this was too late. My reproductive endocrinologist tells me that he wishes he could see most of his patients in their twenties or early thirties. However, during my late twenties and early thirties, I was deep in pediatric residency and pediatric critical care fellowship training and was focused on the demands of the training programs. While career development and female representation in medicine are imperatives, we must plan for the reality of increasing risks of infertility over time.

Based on my experience and what I have learned, a reasonable time to evaluate one's wishes for a family while training in medicine and to pursue consultation with a reproductive endocrinologist is in one's mid-to-late twenties. Also, this is an optimal time for fertility preservation by egg cryo-preservation (freezing) to increase your chances of success. During residency or fellowship, if you do not have a family plan and have not preserved your fertility, I strongly suggest you do so at this time in your career.

For those in training who wish to explore fertility preservation options, discuss your wishes with your program director, graduate medical education representative, or dean if you feel comfortable. Open discussion creates a normalized conversation, which is the foundation for ongoing communication surrounding appropriate time off, understanding your insurance benefits, and finding support as you pursue fertility preservation. If you do not feel comfortable discussing this with your program director or division leader, perhaps find a trusted mentor to help you find resources.

For early-career physicians, discussion with your division director or clinic partners may be required to assist with the necessary time it takes to pursue fertility treatments. Sharing with a trusted coworker at your place of work may also help decrease the burden. However, this is not necessary, and assuredly many have accomplished fertility treatments without informing colleagues. As an early-career physician, it is important that you address your family-building goals and therefore understand your own fertility. I feel it is vital that every physician or physician-in-training considering a family should be empowered with the information contained in this guide to help anticipate and navigate the process.

As stated previously, I would encourage everyone in medicine with a desire to have a family and without current family plans to seek consultation and guidance before the age of thirty. Data for those in their mid-thirties and older shows clear drops in ART success every couple of years. The Society for Assisted Reproductive Technology (SART) reported in 2021 that the percentage of success for a live birth per egg retrieval utilizing ART for those under thirty-five is 44.5 percent, for those ages thirty-five through thirty-seven, it is 32.4 percent, for those ages thirty-eight through forty, it is 20.2 percent, and for those ages forty-one through forty-two, it is 9.6 percent.[14] Thus, if you are over thirty, know you want or may want (more) children, and currently don't have a family plan, research your local reproductive endocrinology clinics and schedule an appointment as soon as possible. See Chapter 6 on *Where to Start-Fertility Treatments* to understand important characteristics of a clinic.

While there are incredibly personal factors that go into the timing of building one's family, the biology that dictates our ability to fulfill our own personal timing is less forgiving. Awareness and recognition of this is the first step in taking control of your future.

4

Maintaining Preventative Health Care

As a member in the medical profession with unusual time demands and shift work, it may be difficult to attend to one's preventative health care. However, there are several health considerations that may affect your fertility, whether you are pursuing natural conception or ART. As part of the ART process, you will be screened for a variety of infectious diseases early in your fertility work-up. These include, but might not be limited to, hepatitis, HIV, and other common sexually transmitted diseases. Staying up-to-date on vaccine-preventable diseases is important to consider in the event you are exposed to these diseases while undergoing ART procedures. If an infectious disease is identified, it may need to be treated or further evaluated before starting the fertility treatments. Chlamydia and gonorrhea, for example, cause infertility and can affect developing fetuses.

For those over forty or who have increased breast cancer risk, mammograms are recommended. Your ART physician may request or require a mammogram without evidence of malignancy before you proceed with your fertility treatments.

Your annual well-woman exams including cervical exam, Pap smear, and breast exam are essential. In my 30's, I began having abnormal Pap smears. These were followed up by a colposcopy, or a small biopsy of the cervix, to look for pre-cancer or cancer cells. Every colposcopy was either negative or showed low-grade abnormal cells (dysplasia). When I was thirty-seven, I was tired of colposcopies, so I asked my physician for a LEEP, or loop electrosurgical excision procedure. This procedure takes a small loop wire and cuts off the very top layer of the cervix to remove abnormal cells. I thought I was being proactive, and this would solve having to undergo further colposcopies in the future. While this ultimately couldn't have been farther from the truth, I am so grateful I advocated for it.

When I received my results from the LEEP, I was diagnosed with cervical adenocarcinoma *in situ* (AIS). This is often still considered pre-cancer; however, it is less common than other forms of cervical dysplasia and more challenging to monitor and treat. AIS is associated with skip lesions higher up in the cervix that are not contiguous with other lesions, so finding the end or margin of the abnormal cells is less straightforward. My LEEP had not removed the margin of this lesion, and thus, I sought the guidance of a gynecology oncologist. He immediately scheduled a cone biopsy (conization) for me, which resects higher up in the cervix in a cone shape. In addition to the identified AIS, there still was a risk of more advanced lesions higher up and, with that, a risk of metastasis, which is something no one wants to consider. I underwent that cone biopsy procedure about six weeks after the LEEP.

After the cone biopsy, I went about my usual day-to-day life after a short recovery period. I was advised to take a "couple of days off." I found that even after four days off, it was still difficult to return to the busy routine of an ICU shift. But the reality of returning to normalcy was, as I remember very vividly, abruptly torn away when I saw the results of that biopsy. My margins for the AIS lesion were still not clear, meaning there was still disease higher in the cervix. I scheduled another cone biopsy six weeks after the first. At that time, I was choosing to undergo repeat procedures to remove affected tissue but was not pursuing the gold standard hysterectomy procedure. This was an attempt to salvage my ability to carry a pregnancy on my own. Between procedures, I added in more yoga to be intentional about regaining my strength and tending to my mental health. It was an early experience that shaped my approach to recovery for many more procedures to come. Finding your method to recover mentally and physically from procedures is important.

After the second cone biopsy, I finally had clear margins. I then visited a high-risk obstetrician to have an evaluation of whether my cervix would remain competent after all these procedures and was told that the chances were good for me to carry a full-term pregnancy. And so began my journey of attempting to conceive and carry my own child. This decision was when I first understood that Choice Moms or Single Moms by Choice were a group I was hoping to join. This group is made up of women who are not romantically partnered and seek to parent via sperm or embryo donors, adoption or fostering. I found https://www.singlemothersbychoice.org to have nice discussions for those thinking about, planning for or already parenting as a single mom by choice. There are also several podcasts and books on the topic. I have listened to the "Single Mom Mindset" podcast and have found a variety of applicable topics.

I tell this story to ensure that all women, whether considering fertility or not, attend to their own preventative health care. You must help yourself before you can help anyone else. My experience with AIS was the first of many opportunities to learn about giving myself the space and grace to recover. This isn't intuitive to many physicians, and we often must be encouraged to attend to our health. Do not feel guilty about making the time to call your personal physicians and go to your appointments. It will not only help you be up to date as you begin your fertility journey, but as I have shown in my case, it is also not hyperbole to say that making that appointment may save your life.

5

Explaining Fertility Terminology

Assisted Reproductive Technology utilizes medical procedures and medications to address infertility, and it includes all procedures where oocytes (eggs) and sperm are manipulated outside of the body.[1] The ART process includes, but is not limited to, medications and procedures to retrieve eggs and sperm.

Reproductive endocrinologists may preliminarily assess female fertility by measuring the anti-mullerian hormone (AMH) amongst other hormones. The AMH is generated by small egg follicles that house immature eggs; so, the higher the number, the higher one's ovarian reserve. The AMH level can give a sense of how successful the egg retrieval process for "freezing your eggs" will be. Your physician should share your estimated chances of having a successful pregnancy based on your age and personal risk factors; the CDC also has a calculator you may use to determine percentages on your own.[15]

Egg retrieval involves seven to ten days of ovarian stimulation medications, which are most commonly injectable medications. Monitoring your response to this regime is accomplished by frequent blood draws and ovarian ultrasounds. This monitoring helps you ensure that your hormone levels are responding appropriately to stimulation and the ovarian antral follicles are growing to an appropriate size. The antral follicle count is the number of egg-containing follicles in your ovaries; the effect of the follicle count on the probability of a successful pregnancy is outlined in Figure 1 given below. Hormone levels and the antral follicle count are the primary factors that contribute to how successful a retrieval may be. It is possible to have your retrieval canceled if your hormones and follicle count do not respond appropriately.

Figure 1. Interpreting the Follicle Count Seen in Ultrasounds during Stimulation Phase

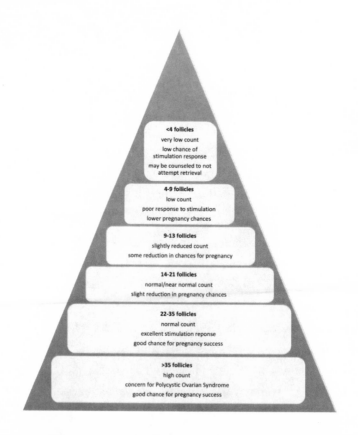

Figure adapted from: Advanced Fertility Center of Chicago.
https://advancedfertility.com/infertility-testing/antral-follicle-counts/

Your clinic will use the hormone levels and follicle counts to determine the optimal day for your egg retrieval, but you will not know this date until the last week of your stimulation. You will need to be flexible on those days, for me it was a three-day window, to be able to undergo the retrieval at your most optimal time. A procedure is then performed to retrieve mature eggs and cryopreserve (freeze) them. Each sequence of events for ovarian stimulation through retrieval is commonly called a cycle. The path to obtaining sperm is usually medication- and procedure-free; however, there are circumstances that are exceptions to this.

There are two common paths following egg retrieval. One path is that eggs are cryopreserved (often referred to as "freezing eggs") after retrieval. The other path is that eggs may be fertilized with sperm (either from a partner, known donor or a sperm bank) in the ART clinic to produce embryos, and this is often referred to as IVF, or in *vitro fertilization*. Embryos may also then be cryopreserved. It is quite common in modern ART that embryos are tested for genetic anomalies, and the test results are usually returned in approximately two weeks.

In comparison to IVF, intrauterine insemination (IUI) involves ovarian stimulation medication, monitoring ovulation, and the uterine lining with ultrasounds, and then the subsequent insertion of the sperm into the uterus. It is cheaper and more non-invasive.

Although I am a physician, most of the vocabulary and processes I experienced were unfamiliar to me. The vocabulary that I was familiar with in mainstream culture was called something else in the ART world. Below are some valuable online and print resources that were helpful to me personally as well as useful while writing this guide.

Online Resources

1. The American Society of Reproductive Medicine
2. National Infertility Association
3. Infertility IQ
4. Society for Advanced Reproductive Technology

Books

1. *It Starts with Egg* by Rebecca Fett

2. *The Underwear in My Shoe: My Journey Through IVF, Unfiltered* by Brett Russo

Below is a list of common vocabulary used in the fertility specialty, along with how it is frequently referred to in mainstream culture and then a medical definition. A special thank you to Dr. Lauren Weissmann, reproductive endocrinologist and friend, for helping me with the clarity of this table and with many questions along the way!

Table 1. Common Vocabulary in the ART world

Medical Term	Common Abbreviation or Vocabulary	Medical Definition
Anti-Mullerian Hormone	AMH	Produced by egg follicles, indicates your ovarian reserve.
Antral Follicle Count	Egg count	Ultrasound-guided study counts the number of egg-containing follicles in your ovaries. This number can suggest the individual's chances of success in a fertility cycle. * See Figure 1 for what this count may mean for your successes
Embryo Transfer	Implanting or Implantation	Transfer of the embryo made in the laboratory to a uterus. See implantation below for definition.

Medical Term	Common Abbreviation or Vocabulary	Medical Definition
Fresh Cycle		Eggs are retrieved and fertilized immediately without any freezing. This contrasts with freezing eggs, and then fertilizing later after a thaw.
Frozen Cycle		Previously retrieved eggs or embryos are thawed. Eggs can then be fertilized, or embryos can be transferred.
Gestational Carrier	Surrogate	A woman who carries a non-genetically related pregnancy for another woman.[16]
Implantation		The transferred embryo attaches to the wall of the uterine lining.
Infertility	Cannot become pregnant	Inability to conceive after one year of unprotected sex.
Intrauterine Insemination	IUI	The procedure to place sperm inside the uterus to increase chances for fertilization.
In Vitro Fertilization	IVF	The process to combine an egg with sperm in a laboratory setting.

Medical Term	Common Abbreviation or Vocabulary	Medical Definition
Oocyte retrieval (may be followed by cryopreservation)	Egg retrieval (freezing)	Transvaginal procedure to remove eggs from your ovaries.
Ovarian Stimulation	Stim	Medication-induced stimulation of ovaries to grow as many eggs as possible.
Surrogate	Surrogate	A person who donates an egg and carries the pregnancy.

6

Where to Start-
Fertility Treatments

This chapter contains practical information on how to get started when considering fertility treatments. Finding the right ART clinic for you is important. Below is a stepwise approach for gathering information and selecting the best clinic for you.

Contact and Review your Health Insurance

Early on in researching ART clinics, obtain information about insurance coverage for fertility visits, labs, and treatments. You may also seek information about the coverage of egg donors, sperm donors, and/or gestational carriers as applicable. Some clinics will obtain this information on your behalf, but you can obtain it on your own. In 2022, there were twenty states with fertility laws for infertility insurance coverage; however, the scope of these varies widely between states.[17] Therefore, there are thirty states without mandated coverage. You may find that you have no coverage whatsoever; you may have one-time benefits, or you may have coverage for repeat cycles.[17] Recently, the federal government mandated that ART coverage be provided to federal employees with federal insurance. This could assist those with federal employee spouses.

Drug coverage may fall under your health insurance, or you may have separate carriers for your pharmacy needs. Most fertility medications are considered "specialty" drugs. As such, they are quite expensive and can run approximately $3,000 to $6,000 per cycle, depending on your personalized regimen. As with health insurance, you may have no drug coverage, one-time benefits, or repeat-cycle coverage. Many reproductive clinics work with phar-macies for discounts. Discuss with the pharmacy that fills your medications if the clinic discount or your insurance discount is better. My sister used GoodRx® for a discount for some of her medications in this process. If you undergo repeat cycles, you may not use every dose of medication ordered for you; therefore, you may have non-expired doses remaining from previ-ous cycles to use on a future cycle. You may not need a full supply of needles, gauze, or new auto-injector pens for every cycle. Discerning this and taking inventory could save you money on future cycles.

The costs for my first two cycles, including lab work, ultrasounds, procedures, sedation, and cryopreservation of the eggs, were entirely my financial responsibility. This financial burden may be prohibitive, especially during training and early career years. Some clinics may have payment plans. There are also resources referenced for funding support in Chapter 8, *Preparing for Egg Retrieval*. This is not an exhaustive list but contains sources that were recommended to me or that I found in my own reading. In anticipation of these expenses, moonlighting or other increases in revenue-generating activities may be an option for some medical professionals.

Research your Local Clinics

Clinics available for ART may be in your city or may require you to consider nearby cities. Patient reviews of ART practices are easy to locate online. Investigate the success rate for procedures relevant to you at the Soci-ety for ART.[14] Generally, the same information is also found on the CDC's website.[15] The outcome data for varying types of procedures could be quite important to your results, so check the data for clinics in your city or clinics that are a reasonable drive for you.

Determine how the clinic communicates with patients. For example, do they rely on online patient portals, emails, or phone calls? Depending on your own clinical work structure or schedule, it may be nearly impossible to take phone calls during business hours. Frequent back-and-forth communication is required, especially during a cycle, so the communication method needs to be efficient and effective for you. It is imperative that you receive up-to-date instructions during cycles, as you may need to make changes for that same evening's medication dosing or order more medication. If you know of friends and colleagues who have used the local clinics you are considering, check with them about their experiences in the clinics if you are comfortable asking that question. You may also inquire with trusted colleagues if they are aware of any reputable clinics in your town. It will surprise you to know how many people have pursued fertility conversations and/or therapy in your institution and have sought advice in local clinics.

Recent legislative changes have also made it necessary to investigate your state laws on how embryos are viewed. By this I mean, it is unclear how new anti-abortion laws will be interpreted at state and local levels in the future. I do not prescribe to know what any one person's values are on this topic, however it is now important to consider.

Make an Appointment for Consultation

My recommendation is to make an appointment at a fertility clinic as soon as you consider pursuing ART. There are often wait times of up to or more than six months at busy practices. Many months may have elapsed from the time you consider making an appointment to the time you receive initial screening results. Some clinics may offer you the opportunity to move into cancellations, so do not be deterred from your desired clinic if the wait for an initial consultation appointment seems very long. If you have records pertaining to your reproductive health or previous ART, having those available for your consultation is helpful. Consultation is usually combined with orders for lab work and ovarian ultrasounds to evaluate your baseline. These labs and ultrasounds are usually timed with your menstrual cycle and are often separate from your consultation. If you are meeting with more than one clinic, consider doing these tests with your selected clinic only to ensure you minimize cost. When considering your clinic, ask about payment plans or specific resources available if your insurance does not provide full coverage.

Additional Information is Available in "*It Starts with the Egg*," by Rebecca Fett

We do not have much control during IVF treatment, so it is beneficial to understand the process. "*It Starts with the Egg*" has been widely read by patients and reproductive endocrinologists. It is highly evidence-based and discusses a thorough review of the medical literature. I read it, and even after having experienced procedures firsthand, I benefited from reading this book. The book gives some suggestions for lifestyle modifications and supplements that may be helpful in a variety of scenarios and contains a section on male infertility as well. As always, discuss suggested changes with your personal physician.

In Summary

Finding the right clinic and understanding your insurance will go a long way in helping you learn how the process may unfold for you. When I began pursuing fertility options, I was with a reputable center in my city. However, during my journey, a new clinic had opened and entered the Top 10 list, as reported by the CDC. With this information, I changed clinics after my initial two egg retrievals and three IUIs, completing my next two retrievals at a different clinic.

I was able to transfer my five frozen eggs from the first clinic to the new clinic, however this transition was accompanied by doubts. I did not make that decision lightly, but I have been happy with my transition, and I am glad

I made it. Anxiety at many different stages in the entire process can lead you to question your decisions. It is easy to let these questions cycle in your head.

Did I wait too long?

Am I at the right clinic?

Is there more I should be doing?

Is there more the clinic should be doing?

These uncertainties are common, but do not suffer the anxiety alone; share it with a friend, family member, therapist, or even your clinic. Do your best when selecting a clinic with the information available to you at the time and trust your decisions.

7

Intrauterine
Insemination

After my fertility-sparing procedures for adenocarcinoma in situ (AIS), as discussed in Chapter 4, *Maintaining Preventative Health Care*, I returned to my initial ART clinic and completed the preliminary screening again. My first endeavor was to pursue intrauterine insemination, or IUI. This procedure is one of the simplest and involves transferring the sperm via catheter directly into the uterus. A benefit of IUI is that it bypasses the vagina and cervix, where many sperm may be lost. To pursue this option, one can have a partner who will provide the sperm, a known nonromantic donor, or a sperm donor may be used. There are many donor banks across the country and this option may be applicable to those in same sex partnerships, those experiencing male infertility in their partnership or those pursuing being single moms by choice. As someone pursuing being a single mom by choice, I asked for donor bank recommendations from my clinic and from friends who had gone through this process. There are online reviews of clinics as well. I recognized that selecting a donor seemed daunting, so I began by considering what my personal values were in selecting a donor. The donor banks share not only physical and personal attributes such as height, hair and eye color and level of education, but they also include a variety of traits by which to filter. These traits include but are not limited to being carriers for genetic conditions, having history of any health conditions and even whether the donor wears glasses. I set out to consider the following attributes:

What kind of genetic screening has been done, and did that align with my personal carrier status?

What mental health screening has been done?

What blood types are compatible with my blood type?

How many children have been linked to this specific donor?

Was the donor open to being contacted in the future by offspring?

To assist with some of these decisions, I had a donor selection party with my closest friends, mom, and sisters. Each person took a site and applied my selected personal donor traits. Then, working as a group, we narrowed the list of possible donors (as I said, I am task-oriented, and others may choose to take a less methodical approach). I took the few remaining donors and poured over their profiles. I ultimately made my final decision while on a family trip. We had just returned from a lovely day out on the water, and I re-read the profiles with my mom, sisters, and sister-in-law. One shared a story of his family out on a boat, so I selected that donor because it was so closely aligned with our recent family outing. While this sperm donor did not ultimately lead to a pregnancy, the process I used made it a positive and less lonely experience.

During the preparation time, ensure you consult with your clinic to determine the number of donor vials needed, and then have your selection shipped directly to the clinic. If you have a partner or known donor who is providing the sperm, they will provide the sample fresh on the day of the procedure. The collection of the sperm sample was formerly performed solely in the ART clinics, but it is now possible for some to obtain the sample at home and then drive it to the clinic.

The clinic works to schedule medications and appointments to sync with your personal menstrual cycle. This process can include oral medications, intravaginal suppositories, and frequent ultrasounds to monitor the uterine lining and follicles. The process may cost $1000-$2000 per completed monthly cycle, in addition to the cost of donor sperm if needed. Side effects vary throughout this experience. I experienced headaches and fatigue as my major symptoms; however, mood swings, nausea, and bloating are also common.[18]

When your uterine lining and hormones reach optimal levels, you will be scheduled for a "trigger" shot that you will likely be asked to self-administer into the skin around your belly button. This is intended to mature your eggs. You will then present yourself to the clinic a day or so later, where the selected sperm is transferred into your uterus. This is performed without any medications for pain or discomfort. The transfer causes some cramping, and you are advised to remain still for ten to fifteen minutes. Thereafter, there were no work restrictions given to me. I went back to work on Christmas Day after my first IUI and participated in a normal ICU day. The anticipatory guidance for returning to work does not always align with women in medicine, in a job with physical demands, or for those with preexisting conditions, such as endometriosis. I also validate that some people are just fine going back to work, even in a high-intensity setting. However, if doing this again, I would consider not returning to work or doing physically demanding activities the same day of IUI, understanding it is challenging to reconcile the timing of the procedure with a full clinical schedule either in or out of the hospital.

After the procedure, you wait fourteen days for the results. The time until the test is mentally challenging. You will continue to take the same precautions as you would if you were pregnant, such as abstaining from alcohol and avoiding strenuous workouts. And you will not know if you should start planning for a baby or for the next round of treatment. I took a pregnancy test at home; however, some clinics may have you come in for confirmatory blood work. When the indicator of "Not Pregnant" appeared, I would share a screenshot of the indicator with close family and friends each time, and that is all I would say about it. They lovingly gave me the space to not talk about it, knowing that it was difficult to see the result. I went through this procedure and process three times; each time, it was unsuccessful. During the last cycle, I had a very clear moment where I thought that I didn't want to do this anymore after experiencing the physical and emotional drain of consecutive IUI cycles. I took that as a sign to take a break from the hormones and poking and prodding to consider my next steps.

After several months though, I had not decided what my next steps would be. By this time, I was nearly two years out from my original diagnosis of cervical AIS. By chance or fate, I had dinner with a friend, who shared her story of uterine cancer and how she had to undergo chemotherapy. I reflected upon my own situation and the knowledge that the ultimate treatment for my diagnosis was a hysterectomy. I talked with another gynecology oncologist, who confirmed my concerns about AIS being a tricky diagnosis, and two years was her recommendation for how long to wait for the definitive curative surgery. With that information, I made an appointment with my own gynecology oncologist to consult about a hysterectomy. The night after my appointment, when I decided to have the hysterectomy, I went to a Maggie Rogers concert and again tried to forget what this meant for my future fertility journey. I would never carry a pregnancy for my own child. But several months later, after an amazing trip with my sisters, I underwent the procedure. This definitively limited my path to motherhood even further by making a gestational carrier or surrogate necessary if I wanted to pursue options outside of adoption.

This guide is not meant to focus on AIS or the treatments thereof; however, it is part of my story and has very much influenced the path I have been on. The remainder of the chapters discuss the therapies available to me after a hysterectomy. Many who turn to IVF for fertility assistance and those who cannot carry a pregnancy due to other medical conditions, may find these chapters helpful. Often, this path begins with the need for an egg retrieval, and that is where the next few chapters will focus.

8

Preparing for Egg Retrieval

There are many reasons one may turn to IVF, including failed IUI, the need to use a gestational carrier or surrogate, or parental genetic concerns. The planning and preparation phase for an IVF cycle may last for months. The first phase is to undergo evaluation and plan to retrieve your eggs. Between the time you make your consultation appointment and enter the IVF cycle, it may take six to twelve months or more. The wait time at many clinics for a consultation is long, and the wait to undergo laboratory and ultrasound testing adds time. Following this, scheduling the actual IVF cycle may take months, based on availability at your clinic. I was, at first, surprised at how lengthy this process can be and was not psychologically prepared for the toll it would take. Knowing what to expect in subsequent cycles helped ease some of the stress. This chapter is intended to give you some ideas on how to prepare for your egg retrieval cycle.

For egg preservation or freezing, there is a preparation phase, a medication-induced egg stimulation phase, and a procedural retrieval phase. We will focus on the preparation phase in this chapter. After your baseline labs and ultrasound to monitor your hormones and follicle counts are complete, your physician may consult on how successful your retrieval is likely to be. As a reminder, a chart in Chapter 5, *Explaining Fertility Terminology* shares the number of follicles and suggests expectations for success. A higher AMH and follicle count is desirable. With this information, your physician prepares a personalized medication plan, and you decide on the timing of your cycle and subsequent egg retrieval based on clinic availability and your schedule. Some clinics will put patients on birth control for the month prior to a cycle. If you have an intra-uterine device (IUD), this will need to be removed. The stimulation phase will proceed once your medication regimen has been planned and you have scheduled your cycle dates with the clinic. The stimulation phase is when your injections begin. The time from starting your injections to egg retrieval is typically between seven and thirteen days.

Prepare yourself for the cycle by attending to your health. Now is the time to practice good self-care. Your ovaries are sensitive to stress and sleep deprivation, so take time to focus on sleep habits. Be intentional about a good sleep schedule. Be mindful to practice regular physical activity at your usual intensity. While being at a healthy weight is important during fertility treatment, this is not the time to partake in strenuous exercise you are not accustomed to. Limit alcohol and sugar.[19,20] Treat yourself to activities that are relaxing for you. Read a book, get a massage, have a pedicure, or settle in for a good movie. Acupuncture is often discussed as an adjunct to fertility treatment. The data on this is mixed; however, if an acupuncture treatment forces you to slow down and be restful for an hour per treatment, it may be helpful from that perspective alone.[21,22] It is often recommended that you begin acupuncture treatments several months before the retrieval so finding a clinic may also be on your task list. Some clinics will advertise that they specialize or have providers who focus on fertility specifically. Again, friends or coworkers may have had experiences with acupuncture during their fertility journeys and can be helpful with referrals.

When deciding on the timing of your egg retrieval cycle, consider your schedule carefully. The cycles require up to four or five ultrasound and lab appointments before the retrieval itself; thus, your clinical workday could be impacted. Consider the following questions as applicable to you.

Do you work in a clinic where you can delay the start of your appointments?

Are you in a hospital setting, and can you trade shifts or take shifts later in the day?

Do you have night shifts or traditional call schedules as part of your usual clinical time, and can you limit these or trade them?

I was on clinical service in the hospital for nearly all my cycles until the last one. No one told me to try to limit my work schedule; however, many people who have been through several cycles have learned this over time. For my last cycle, I had one night shift going into the cycle but was on administrative time the remainder of the cycle, and this experience was much easier for me physically and mentally. I recommend trading out of night calls during the stimulation phase for my trainees. Therefore, if you are scheduling a cycle, I suggest speaking to your program or division director and identifying what flexibility is available to you. Do not be reticent to alter your schedule.

There may be nutritional supplements recommended to support your cycle. At a minimum, you will be on a good prenatal vitamin, and you should start this at least by when you make your consultation appointment to ensure several months of adequate supplementation. The types of other supplements you take depend very much on your baseline situation, age and your physician's preferences. By this, I mean that if you are older and/or have had multiple failed cycles, you are likely to be taking more ovarian health supplements. Examples of some supplements commonly used are Açai, Coenzyme Q, Melatonin, and DHEA (dehydroepiandrosterone).[23, 24, 25, 26] There is data concerning the use of these supplements, and you may be placed on some of them as appropriate by age recommendations when you schedule your cycle dates. I found it helpful to set a daily reminder on my phone to ensure I was compliant with taking these supplements. I also learned to pack my supplements in advance when on busy clinical shifts so that I could take the correct ones at the correct times. If you work night shifts or take long inhouse calls, you may wonder when to take your melatonin, as this is usually an evening sleep supplement. There does not seem to be a consensus on whether you should skip melatonin or take it during the day while you sleep. I admittedly sometimes skipped it and sometimes took it during the day.

Consider telling your friends or family members when you are undertaking the cycle. The process is mentally, physically, and socially difficult. The physical toll of going through all the injections and hormonal changes is serious and affects your day heavily. Socially, it feels isolating that you are going through something so all-consuming, yet most people around you are unaware. Thus, having someone know that you might need support during this time is beneficial. I found it helpful to have friends at work know as well, but it is intensely personal with whom one wishes to share this experience. I have an amazing family and friend support network, but I found that seeing a therapist helped me process my grief and fear along the way. There are also specialized reproductive therapists who can provide counseling during this time. Your ART clinic should have some recommendations for local therapists.

Lastly, plan for the financial burden. Understanding the financial strain in advance is well worth the time, so you are not surprised by a bill or payment requirement. By now, you know what your insurance will cover as well as the estimated cost that the clinic will charge. Likely, a retrieval cycle with IVF will cost on the order of $10,000-$20,000. This may require you to cut back on other expenses while you wait for your cycle. Some take extra moonlighting shifts to supplement their income and cover this expense. Some have taken out loans. A recent paper also reviewed some resources available to medical students with encouraging results overall; however, only one school provided coverage for elective fertility preservation such as egg freezing![27] Below are a few resources that are recommended; however, as a disclaimer, I have not used them personally. Freeze by Co is a company that may pay for your egg freezing if you donate half your retrieval and has served medical student graduates previously. Shady Grove Fertility is exclusive to surgical specialty trainees and is geographically specific but an additional resource.

Financial Resources

Ally

https://www.ally.com/personal-loans/medical-loans/fertility-financing

Future Family

www.futurefamily.com

Lending Club

www.lendingclub.com/trypatientsolutions/fertility

Freeze by Co

https://www.cofertility.com

Shady Grove Fertility

https://www.shadygrovefertility.com/treatments/egg-freezing/
surgical-residents-program/

After you navigate all the preparation time, you will be ready for your scheduled stimulation and retrieval cycle. We will review this phase further in the next chapter.

9

What to Expect during the Stimulation Phase

The egg retrieval stimulation phase is quite intense, and planning is vital. Approximately one month before your intended cycle start date, you will work with your clinic to order your medications. Depending on your drug insurance coverage, you may go through your insurance company's pharmacy, or you may work with a company your clinic contracts with. Often, the clinics have discounts in place, so if your insurance does not provide benefits, the clinic discount may be the best course of action. If you experience repeat cycles, remember to take inventory of all the non-expired medications and supplies and only order what you need.

You may need to be present to sign at the time of delivery of the medications. Then you will need time to organize them into refrigerated and non-refrigerated storage immediately. It is important to anticipate this time in your schedule or arrange for someone to be available to receive the delivery. At this time, or even prior to delivery, there should be injection videos or tutorials available for you to watch. Even with a medical background, it is important to watch the videos because each medication differs in delivery and dosing. I often kept printouts of how to administer each medication handy at my injection location, so I could easily reference them and verify the delivery. Some medications arrive with an auto-injector pen, which is a device with preloaded doses and a spring-loaded syringe. I personally prefer auto-injectors and wish they were supplied with all medications, as the doses can be easily measured out. However, some medications require you to mix the provided solutions and then draw up the prescribed dose. Most injections are subcutaneous and are given in the area around your belly button. Injections may be given once or twice a day, depending on your personal regimen. If you are injecting multiple medications a day, it is again helpful to be familiar with the delivery systems in advance.

You will need to carefully plan the timing of your daily injections. Commonly, injections are recommended to be administered between six and nine o'clock, and depending on your regimen, this may be once or twice a day, in the morning and evening. Often, those who may have more difficulty stimulating their follicles will have injections twice daily. If you have injections twice a day, you will want to do them at the same time in the morning and evening. If you have daily injections once a day, then the same time every night is important. The injection schedule becomes challenging for anyone working in a clinical medical setting. Investing in a medication cooler will help you organize your medications to take to work with you. Consider a cooler that can also accommodate an ice pack so you can ice your injection site as you deem necessary. Some medications do burn more upon delivery; thus, the recommendation for ice is a common trick to alleviate discomfort.

Don't rush injections and limit any distractions during injection time, especially if you are at work or tired at the end of the day. Mistakes in drawing up medicines can lead to errors in medication delivery. Some common mistakes are inappropriate or inaccurate mixing or not fully inserting a needle into the syringe leading to medication leaking when you inject. After several days of injections, you will be more accustomed to the process. But keep the instructions for each medication in the location you inject, so you can quickly reference details during each injection. Now a moment for a true confession: I say this after having made many mistakes over the course of several cycles. If you make a mistake, call or message your clinic, and they will instruct you on any alterations to future doses or assist with ordering more medication.

Side effects from these medications vary by individual. Bloating and abdominal fullness are nearly universal as your ovaries grow. After several cycles, a nurse commented that we are growing the ovaries from the size of almonds to grapefruits and this analogy stuck with me forever after that. Additional symptoms may include, but are not limited to, fatigue, headache, and gastrointestinal distress. You cannot use pain relievers like Advil or Aleve during this time, so those who suffer migraines or other pain symptoms may need an alternative plan. Consider limiting your personal engagements, as you may not feel up to them, and scheduling fewer versus canceling later could decrease your stress. Travel during this stimulation phase and after your retrieval is not advised, as your physician will want you to be geographically close in the event any complications occur. Physical activity will be limited to low-impact activities such as walking. High-impact activity, core exercises, weightlifting, and yoga are discouraged. This is due to a risk for ovarian torsion, or twisting, of the ovary. Ovarian torsion is a medical emergency that could lead to the loss of the ovary. Sexual intercourse is also discouraged. Pushing your hydration to at least two liters a day is commonly discussed, so ensure you have a water bottle with you at work. Ovarian hyperstimulation syndrome is a risk of ovarian stimulation. This is when the ovaries can become large and painful and, in severe cases, can lead to hospitalization.[28] Ovarian Hyperstimulation Syndrome is rare and estimated to occur in less than 2 percent of patients in stimulation.[28]

As already discussed, modify your clinical schedule as much as possible. Consider taking vacation or sick days as the day for egg retrieval nears. There may be five or more clinic appointments during the stimulation phase that must be done on certain mornings and are inflexible in scheduling. At each appointment, lab tests and ovarian ultrasounds are performed to monitor hormone levels and your follicle count. The follicle count will tell you how many follicles may develop and be retrieved as mature eggs. Not all follicles will mature, so calibrate your expectations with this in mind. Typically, follicles that grow to a certain size are considered promising for viability at retrieval. Monitoring appointments are commonly in the morning, and then the results of those studies are communicated with you later in the day. As we discussed in Chapter 6, *Where to Start-Fertility Treatments*, effective communication with your clinic now becomes imperative. These results may be associated with a change to your medications or even a need to order more, and this must be done immediately.

As retrieval time approaches, your physician will determine when you are to administer the "trigger" injection. The trigger injection is intended to mature developing eggs and induce ovulation for retrieval day. Mature eggs are required for fertilization; thus, harvesting the greatest number of mature eggs is the ultimate objective. The trigger injection will be specifically timed, and it is important to adhere to your specified time as your retrieval time is based upon the prescribed trigger time. The trigger injection is often different in its administration. It may be an intramuscular injection using a longer needle and is often placed in the buttock. This administration is tricky to do on your own the first time. Many people accomplish these injections without help. I however, asked my sister for assistance, and she kindly obliged. As a data analyst, I knew she would be extremely precise in following the injection instructions, and she certainly was. The memories of her drawing with a sharpie on my backside while my other sister told jokes are priceless and provided some much need laughing during an otherwise difficult process.

You are almost ready now for the retrieval day, which we will discuss in the next chapter. Stay vigilant concerning your rest, hydration, and avoidance of strenuous activity until retrieval. It can become exhausting close to retrieval time, and you can lose focus. Remember your goals and have plans on how to stay accountable to your regimen. A romantic partner can assist with this or consider sharing your plans with a trusted friend or family member to support you through such a strict regimen.

I O

What to Expect on Egg Retrieval Day and After

The date for the egg retrieval is initially provided by your clinic using a range of days. Thus, it can be difficult to plan for work obligations because you will not know your retrieval day until the week of retrieval. You will need the day of retrieval and the following day off work at a minimum. During my first retrieval, I was not advised to have the following day off of work obligations. I became febrile the night of my procedure and could not work the next day. Since then, my second clinic has advised me to not work the day after a retrieval. I took this one step further and ensured I had at least two days off of clinical work for subsequent retrievals. My work in the ICU, and that of many physicians, does not lend itself to "taking it easy" when you go back to work. You may have to be ready to stand or walk for twelve hours at a time, and perhaps even run, to get to an emergency.

On the day of retrieval, you will arrive at your clinic's procedure suite at the designated time after having not eaten or drunk anything since the night before. You also will need a trusted adult to drive you home after the retrieval. You will have an IV as a monitored anesthetic is administered for this procedure, and thus, you will be evaluated by an anesthesia practitioner.

The procedure uses a transvaginal approach to insert a needle into your ovaries and retrieve the eggs. After your procedure, you will recover at the clinic or procedure site for a short time, and when you are ready, the trusted adult will drive you home. This trusted adult may be recommended to be present with you for twenty-four hours afterwards. I did need some help post procedure as I experienced some cramping and fatigue, which are common. I also felt abdominal wall soreness after my retrievals, which is not frequently discussed by clinics or in the anticipatory materials provided.

Sometime during your procedure day, it may be before you are discharged or later in the day that the embryologist will inform you about the number of eggs that were mature and viable for freezing or fertilization. This can be an emotional time for you if the number is not what you had hoped for. It can also be a relief to those who have a successful retrieval and only need one cycle to store an adequate number of eggs. Personally, my first two cycles yielded five eggs each, my third yielded three eggs but my fourth and final cycle yielded no mature eggs. Recovering from anesthesia after my final retrieval and receiving this news was sad. My mom and I cried quietly in the recovery room together, knowing this was likely the last of my retrievals and that my personal fertility window was likely over.

If you are freezing only eggs, your cycle is complete when you know the number of mature eggs that will be frozen. Then you are on to recovery. Again, you should have at least one to two days off from most activities after retrieval. Your activity restrictions, including sexual activity and physical fitness, often continue until your next menstrual cycle. This is because, after retrieval, your ovaries take time to shrink to their normal size. Even after activity restrictions are lifted, people often share that they don't feel quite normal. This can be due to ongoing bloating, gastrointestinal symptoms, and regaining strength lost during activity restrictions. Give yourself some grace to recover at your own pace. I was never the one to pop up the next day after any procedure and feel ready for work or any other activity. Pushing yourself too early can lengthen the recovery.

With freezing eggs, they remain frozen until you decide to thaw and use the eggs in the future. The cost of initial storage is often accounted for in the initial cycle cost. However, there may be annual fees if eggs are stored for longer than a year. The payment schedule for storage should be made clear to you prior to your procedure.

If your intended goal with this egg retrieval is to fertilize the eggs for a full IVF cycle immediately, fertilization will occur the day of retrieval. I fertilized my second egg retrieval round, which yielded five eggs. You will then be notified over the coming days about the number of eggs that were fertilized, and which embryos then matured to the blastocyst stage. A blastocyst is a rapidly dividing cell group that can develop the embryo and has the necessary structures to support it.[29] The maturation process to the blastocyst stage takes approximately five days. Not all fertilized eggs will make it to this point. I had one embryo make it to this stage in my first round of IVF. After maturation, there is an opportunity for genetic testing of those blastocysts. Genetic testing is commonly done prior to embryo transfer to you or to a gestational carrier. Genetic testing, however, may not be mandatory, and not everyone chooses to do the testing. The process of retrieval, fertilization, and then maturation of embryos is also stressful as you wait to see how many you (and your partner, as applicable) were able to obtain. If you obtain the embryo's genetic profile, the results will take several weeks. The results can be joyful or disappointing. My one embryo at this stage was not genetically healthy, and so I was left with nothing after my second round. With four total IVF cycles across many years and two clinics, I obtained only two healthy embryos. Once you understand how many healthy embryos there are, the process of determining the timing of an embryo transfer to you or a gestational carrier can begin.

Some of you may choose to keep your embryos frozen until the timing in your life is desirable or you may proceed toward embryo transfer immediately. The time from scheduling your egg retrieval to transfer may require several months. Refer to Chapter 13, *Embryo Transfer* if you are planning this journey.

This process has now likely taken a physical and emotional toll on you. Again, allow some space and grace for yourself to recover. Make a schedule to return to any desired fitness activities. Perhaps make an appointment with your therapist or a reproductive therapist to debrief how you feel at this point. Reconnect with your partner or have a relaxing meal or a chat with a trusted friend or family member who knows what you have been going through. Should you be done with treatments for a while, planning to continue with embryo transfer or another round of retrieval, you will need to spend some time tending to your needs!

II

Egg Donors and Sperm Donors

If IUI or IVF are unsuccessful or a single person or same sex couple wish to pursue ART, there are several additional existing options. Egg donors and sperm donors are available and are becoming more easily accessible over time. Additionally, donor embryos are also available. I do not have much experience with this and the laws surrounding embryos are becoming more heterogenous so I will not spend time on this topic. However, regarding egg donors, the donor undergoes the same treatment described previously for egg retrieval, freezing, and then storing the eggs with local or national registries. Sperm donors will donate at any number of clinics, with the process for donation being much easier without the need for medications, injections, or medical procedures.

For those who cannot carry a pregnancy, have been unsuccessful in IUI or IVF, or are male same-sex couples, egg donors may be an option of interest. Donors are often housed in national or local registries and can be perused to see if the traits and characteristics you value are identified in a donor. Eggs can be selected from cycles already completed (frozen) or you may wait for a donor to complete an upcoming egg retrieval cycle (fresh).

The number of eggs available to a prospective parent may vary by registry but is often around five or six as the base number. This number of frozen eggs, or a cohort, can cost $10,000 at a minimum and $30,000 in some banks. The live birth success rate with fresh cycles has historically been considered to be higher however the success gap between fresh and frozen may be closing. A fresh cycle may cost even more as you pay for the entire IVF cycle for the donor. The most recent difference between live birth success rates varies by source but is reported in 2021 by the Society of ART at 41.4 percent for fresh eggs and 39.1 percent for frozen eggs.[14] There are several pros and cons for each type of cycle and further discussion with your ART specialist can help you determine what is best for you. It is also important to understand how many eggs will be in your donor cohort and if there will be a blastocyst (commonly shortened to "blast") guarantee. This guarantee generally states that if no mature embryo, known as a blastocyst, is produced, you may proceed with an additional round of IVF at no or reduced cost.

As a single parent by choice, a female same-sex couple, or if a partner has male infertility, you may need to select a sperm donor. There are far more sperm banks nationally than there are egg banks. Your ART clinic may recommend certain banks that they have worked closely with, feel comfortable with and/or have had good success with. I tried to use those recommendations to make the process as easy as possible for the clinic's embryology laboratory. A consultation with your clinic about how many vials you will need is advised so you don't select a donor and come to find later that the donor is out of inventory, should you find yourself needing more vials.

I personally have used the Seattle Sperm Bank several times. Other popular and vetted sperm banks are listed in a variety of places, including https://www.ivfauthority.com. These banks have a variety of filters to select your race or ethnicity, physical attributes, and genetic or mental health screening. Often, there are pictures of the donors as children as well as voice samples. Personality and/or mental health screenings may also be available. Each vial of sperm can vary in cost, but $600-$1,000 is common.

For either egg donors or sperm donors, their profiles may be able to be downloaded from the sites so that you have the information available for any children born with a donor. I would recommend doing this upon the purchase of sperm or eggs, so that you don't lose access to this information. Children born via ART will likely have questions about donor history, and this is a tangible way to help them understand their identity. Assisting your children with identity awareness is commonly recommended in both adoption and ART donor guidance.

The selection of donors is an extremely personal choice. Determine what you are looking for and try to adhere to your preferences during the process. Because I had multiple IVF cycles over many years and in two different clinics, I selected three different sperm donors in the process. However, I kept my personal values for donors consistent throughout each selection process. This is not to say you can't change your mind about different parameters as you travel this journey! I just encourage you to have a good sense of what is important to you during the selection process.

Good luck with your selection!

12

Gestational Carriers and Surrogates

Because I had a hysterectomy, I learned about gestational carriers as an option available to me. When adoption proved difficult, I pursued this option more aggressively (more on adoption in Chapter 14, *What About Adoption?*). Gestational carriers, commonly known as surrogates, are people with a uterus who carry a pregnancy for another person. A traditional surrogate utilizes their egg and carries the baby, while a gestational carrier provides the latter of those services without any genetic relation. Finding a gestational carrier (GC) or surrogate is often difficult and can take a year or more to be matched by an agency. There are agencies available to assist in this process, or you may make a private arrangement. Your ART clinic should have resources for finding a GC or surrogate. The experience I describe is for the United States, as other countries have different laws surrounding this topic. Additionally, within the United States, regulations vary by state. Consult with your clinic and legal counsel for additional specifics about your state.

A GC or surrogate is often considered if they have carried a prior successful pregnancy, are less than thirty-five years old, and are otherwise generally healthy.

Once you find a GC or surrogate, the carrier will need to be screened for mental and physical health by your ART clinic. There will be lab draws, ultrasounds, and uterine studies. You may be responsible for the cost of this screening, so once again, investigate with your insurance and the insurance of your GC or surrogate. You, as the intended parent(s), IP(s), are also likely to be screened for mental health by a fertility therapist or trained mental health professional prior to entering a legal contract. If the GC or surrogate is married or in a relationship, it is important to ensure the partner is supportive of the plan.

If your GC or surrogate is medically screened as ready for a pregnancy, there will be legal consultation regarding the agreement between the IP(s), the GC or surrogate, and their partner, as applicable. You, your GC, or surrogate will likely have different lawyers. The cost of legal fees for the GC or surrogate is generally the responsibility of the IP(s). These fees can vary; however, for the IP(s) and GC or surrogate fees, combined, one can expect $10,000 or more. The contract itself will discuss compensation as allowed by the state's laws (some states such as Louisiana do not allow GC/surrogate compensation), coverage of any medical fees, and assistance with clothing, childcare, or home cleaning services for the GC or surrogate. Compensation varies by geography but can be expected to be around $15,000 or more, but again, some states do not allow compensation based on their own laws.

Additional issues to consider are the kind of diet you might request your GC or surrogate to follow, activity or travel restrictions, and COVID-19 exposure. While writing this guide in 2022, the addition of pregnancy termination agreements became an even more essential topic to clearly include in the contract as Roe V. Wade was overturned. This has created widely variable access to termination. Doctor visits over the course of the pregnancy and delivery room attendance are also important topics to discuss with your GC or surrogate. An additional piece to consider is the acquisition of a supplemental life insurance policy for the GC or surrogate should there be the untimely death of the GC or surrogate during the pregnancy (an insurance policy can cost several hundred dollars). Once the contract is executed, the ART clinic should be notified. With the signed contract, the plan for initiation of the medications for an embryo transfer may begin.

During this process, a request for full estate planning was also made of me. This allows for financial and guardianship planning for the child should the IP(s) die during pregnancy. These are all unpleasant aspects to consider but necessary for the legal process. The cost of my estate planning was $2,500, but this can certainly vary widely depending on needs, law firm selection, and geography.

I was fortunate to have a GC that I knew. It took a full year from the time we started talking about partnering in the journey to the first transfer. Some of this time was for me to complete my decision making around embryo creation. Some was related to the rounds of IVF and work-up and preparation for my GC. This lengthy time frame was not something she or her husband were anticipating. We could have better set expectations if we had known the length of their commitment. For me, I could not have anticipated how much deep investment I would have in her and her well-being. It was important for me to meet and know her family, and we were free to do this in our independent match. I had lunch with her and her husband prior to our first transfer to ensure I had met him prior to a possible pregnancy (I'll explain more about transfers in the next chapter). At the beginning of each of her cycles, I wanted to let her know I was supportive and validating that this was a big undertaking. For me, I showed this with care packages I sent to her home and always ensured I was available for easy communication. She reciprocated by including me in the process by sending me videos every night at her injection time, with her daughters sometimes joining the routine.

I was privileged in knowing my GC; we chatted nearly every day as we went through the medical/psychological work-up and prepared for transfer. We texted every day of her stimulation phase and multiple times a day after transfer. It has been a once-in-a-lifetime bond that I am extremely grateful for. Currently, my GC and I support other teams with care items in our Etsy Shop, Everyday Fertility. If you are looking for ideas for gifts for your GC/surrogate, yourself or others on your fertility journey with you, check out our co-founded site https://www.etsy.com/shop/EverydayFertility.

13

Embryo Transfer

Each phase of infertility treatment has many steps and learning about each of them is important. The next phase after egg retrieval, fertilization, and the determination of embryo health is to set the time for an embryo transfer. The following discussion regarding embryo transfer is applicable to you as an individual who intends to carry a pregnancy and/or to a gestational carrier (GC) or surrogate.

Preparation for an embryo transfer includes more hormone injections, oral medications, and supplemental estrogen. There are, again, multiple clinic appointments for lab checks and ultrasounds of the uterine lining. All of these must be planned for with the same attention to adhering to the medication regimen and making work schedule accommodations. See Chapter 8, *Preparing for Egg Retrieval,* to review this discussion. The goal of this preparation is to boost estrogen levels and increase the uterine lining to a size that is most hospitable to a transferred embryo. Again, as with egg retrieval, sexual activity should be avoided during this time. The ovaries are not being stimulated during this process; however, strenuous exercise is usually limited.

If the uterine lining achieves the desired depth and maturation during the monitoring phase, then the transfer will be proceed as scheduled. You may have more accuracy around which day your clinic anticipates this being so scheduling your clinical duties can be easier with this procedure. The procedure itself includes catheter transfer of the embryo to the uterus. On transfer day, my GC and I exchanged gifts, and while she has such a generous and creative disposition and, resultantly, is a better gift giver, it was important to me to show my support for her in my own way too. The transfer occurs without anesthesia, but anxiety medication may be prescribed. At my fertility clinic, I was able to watch the embryo be placed in the catheter in the lab and was also able to watch the transfer on ultrasound. I was given a picture of the moment of transfer and of the embryo before transfer. After transferring the embryo, you or your surrogate or GC, will remain still for a short time prior to leaving the clinic. Restrictions provided may vary, some based on the clinic, and could include modified bed rest; however, you or the surrogate or GC will likely need to consider scheduling time off after this procedure as well. There is, then, a waiting period of at least ten days for the pregnancy test. This time can be stressful as you await results and find out if the transfer resulted in pregnancy. The balance between hope and not getting your hopes too high is a challenge. Once the in-office pregnancy test, often referred to as a beta (short for beta-human chorionic gonadotropin), is returned, you can experience the utter joy of a successful transfer or complete heartache for the loss of the embryo. The first transfer to my GC was unsuccessful. I only had two embryos at the beginning of our transfer process, and so the loss of one of them was devastating. It was also disappointing as reported success rates for transfers are approximately 65 percent. The GC had done everything right, yet the transfer did not work. This was emotional for us both in different ways and was the hardest part of the process for her. She had been so positive and so sure the transfer would be successful; it was a hard truth to face that it had been unsuccessful. After so much work to achieve my own pregnancy in the past, this was yet another disappointment. And for a time, I wanted to just quit trying. It took me several months to be able to think about the future and be excited about the next transfer.

Because I only had one embryo remaining, my GC and I decided we would do a cycle that culminated in essentially a uterine biopsy. This is a new study and is commonly called an Endometrial Receptivity Analysis (ERA). The goal is to assess the optimal timing of embryo transfer. My GC graciously agreed to go through an entire cycle of medications, lab draws, and appointments to determine if we needed different timing for the transfer. Results from the ERA showed us that my GC was pre-receptive. One may also be found to be post-receptive or may be found to be optimally timed with standard hormone administration. For us, being pre-receptive meant that her hormone regimen needed to be changed to provide the hormone progesterone for a full twenty-four hours longer. With this information, we proceeded through yet another cycle for her and the embryo transfer.

On the day of the second embryo transfer, knowing this was the last embryo, I initially thought I was handling it well emotionally. However, later that morning, I surprisingly vomited and realized perhaps I was a bit more anxious than I had realized! My GC and I proceeded to the clinic, and she underwent an uneventful transfer. For the next ten days, we were constantly in touch. We shared our hopes, fears, and hurt over the loss of the first embryo, which was a baby girl. We commented on how we were taken off guard by how much we were thinking about our first embryo that didn't implant. And I thought about how hard it must be for those who undergo miscarriages, and my heart broke for all the moms who have had to endure that.

On day ten, my GC went in for her beta test. Of note, some may have a different timeframe that their clinic recommends. There is a range of normal and accepted strategies. But, before I had any idea what day our test would be, I had months earlier scheduled myself to give Grand Rounds out of town, and so I was flying back home while we waited for her results. It was nerve-wracking and emotional, and the day was a blur. I landed and went immediately to my GC's house to wait for the call from the clinic. When we received the call and learned we were pregnant, the emotions flowed. In the following days, tears of joy and excitement, but also of all the grief and loss, came too. These feelings of grief and loss are difficult for most to understand, as they see only the joy of the moment. But all the disappointments, the loss of my own ability to carry a pregnancy, and the loss of my daughter bubbled up as much as the joy did that day. A friend shared her feelings on this same experience poignantly and agreed to be identified as I share her comment next.

"I underestimated the amount of grief, shame and embarrassment that comes along with a failing body. And equally underestimated the amount of gratitude and joy that comes along with finding a stranger to carry your unborn child."

-Lauren Rissman, MD, Pediatric Critical Care and
Palliative Care Physician

On the day my GC and I found out we were pregnant; we both allowed all the feelings to be felt and acknowledged them. And we moved forward day by day.

After the first beta, the level is often checked again to ensure it is going up appropriately. You, your GC, or surrogate, will continue the injections you had been using pretransfer for around eleven total weeks. You, your GC, or surrogate, will be monitored in the ART clinic at first, and then transfer prenatal care to your primary obstetrician if all progresses normally.

There are no words to describe the gratitude I have for my GC. And I am certain that if I were carrying the pregnancy myself as many who read this are hopeful to do, I would feel the same gratitude for being pregnant at the end of this long journey. After six and a half years of fertility treatment, the process gave me what I had wanted all along. But it is not easy, and often people think IVF is a sure thing. I am here to say that for some, it all works out the first time, and that is extraordinary and wonderful. For others, it is a process that takes dedication and perseverance and has truly changed me. But when I got to plan to attend an Ed Sheeran concert with a pregnant GC, it was finally a concert I got to align with a happy and hopeful time.

14

What about Adoption?

Owing to my struggles with health and infertility, a natural option to consider was adoption. People in the media and in everyday conversation commonly say, "Just adopt." I value the role of adoption in building a family, and I also know many people have had positive experiences with adoption. Those who would say "just adopt" have little awareness of how lengthy and emotional the process can be.

I share my experience to assist others with understanding timelines, financial commitments, and what to actually expect. I started the adoption process by asking for some recommendations from friends and friends of friends, and then researched the agencies online. There are agencies that will be geographically local to you, and there are national agencies that work in multiple states. Once you identify some agencies you are interested in, there are some initial fact-finding phone calls and emails. After your interviews with the agencies, you will select one and sign a contract. This contract is usually valid for a year and costs several thousand dollars for the representation. You may then be assigned a contact person who will be your information source going forward.

You will also want to know how the agencies present you and your story to potential birth mothers or parents for consideration. To understand the differences in these approaches, there is some vocabulary to learn. What is a "situation?" A situation is a potential birth mother or birth parents who are making an adoption plan for the child. Some agencies will obtain your personal criteria and show your story to all situations that meet those criteria. Some will ask for your approval in every situation prior to sending your information. This process is very focused on the birth mother and the best option for the future child, as it should be. If a birth mother or parents select you from your submitted information, that is then called a "match."

A full self-reflection of what traits or characteristics you will look for in a possible birth mother as well as in an adoptive child is, in my opinion, essential. The following are not questions that everyone will find applicable to them, and I am not pushing them as necessities to everyone. This too, is an extremely personal process however these are some common questions that arise.

What is important to you?

Will the age of the mother, drug exposure history, or maternal health history be something you consider prior to being considered for a match?

Will you ask for a prenatal history for the baby?

Do you wish to restrict opportunities to a certain geographic location?

Identifying these criteria early and adhering to them was an important aspect for me during the adoption process. I recognize everyone is very different in how they approach this process all these approaches are valid.

There is much that goes into preparation for an adoption. One large part of the preparation phase is the home study. Awareness about the complex and time-consuming process to be "home study approved" is worth noting. The home study process is when a licensed adoption agency evaluates your personal and financial life. The home study may cost $1500 or more to complete. Depending on the agency you choose to sign with, the home study may be completed by them. The home study may need to be done by a local group if your agency is a national agency. The home study agency will run background checks, assess your financial stability, evaluate your physical and mental health, and assess your home. It can feel very invasive to prove your worthiness as a parent to others, but it is necessary, and I understand the need for all the requirements. An additional piece of the home study is the training and education process. The training includes learning how to prepare to parent an adopted child. There are many things to consider, including interracial adoptions, bringing a child into a home where there are already children, and how to prepare for communication with the child concerning adoption over the span of his/her life. The depth of these topics is beyond the scope of this book, but there are several resources available to prepare you and your family as applicable to welcome a child. As an example, my family read *In on It: What adoptive parents would like you to know about adoption*, by Elisabeth O'Toole.

Another piece of adoption preparation is creating a "profile." The profile is meant to give a birth mother a look into your life and, subsequently, the life of their unborn child. There are different services available to assist with creating the profile, and your adoption agency should be able to provide some recommendations. It takes some time to provide a history of your life and to collect photographs to give birth mothers a glimpse into your life. The profile must be completed before you are considered for any potential matching situation.

After your home study and profile are complete, the waiting begins. At first, I received several situations, and I felt encouraged. However, I soon discovered that the number of adoptions overall had been declining in the US, and during the COVID-19 restrictions, there were noticeable continued declines. I was very ready at that time to bring a child into my home; however, that was not my time. At one point, my adoption agency called, and I was surprised because they rarely called. They shared that a baby had already been born near me and asked if I would like to be considered. It was shocking and exciting to know that I might be called to pick up the baby the next day. However, after agreeing to be considered, I did not hear another word about the situation. One must be prepared to go from welcoming a child into their home the next day to never hearing about the baby again.

What happens if you match with a birth mother? The cost can vary widely from $30,000-$60,000. This may cover living expenses and medical expenses for the birth mother and child. Of note, there is an adoption tax credit available to some who meet the requirements for salary eligibility. There are fundraising options your agency may help you with, or you may need to consider a loan.

After the match, you may meet the birth mother in person or have a phone call. Contracts will be signed; however, it will be up to the birth mother to sign the final documents and transfer parenthood to you upon birth. As the adoption is not considered to be final until the birth mother confirms her decision after the birth, there is often a financial risk that is reported if the adoption does not get finalized. Some states have a relatively easy process for adoptive parents after birth; however, some require you to stay in the birth state for a designated period of time, up to weeks after the birth, for the legal process to be completed. There may be additional waiting periods and legal proceedings, again depending on the state.

I learned about flexibility while going through the adoption process, as there was much I could not control. I had to learn to accept those things and know that I was doing my best. I personally struggled with many unknowns in the medical and mental health history provided about birth mothers and their babies however I know this is not the case for many in the adoption journey. I had multiple episodes of communication over this time, sharing that while we could ask questions of the situation, the number of prospective adoptive families was so high that agencies representing birth mothers rarely responded to any questions. I renewed my home study at the one-year mark, but halfway through the second year, I pivoted to working with a gestational carrier and moved down that path.

I still believe in the joy that adoption can bring, and I have several people in my life who are adoptive parents or have adopted children. I see the great value and love in their history, story, and experience. And I know it works well for many. This was just not my journey to motherhood.

15

Now that You Know

After reading my story—about a woman in medicine and her pursuit of a family—what feelings or thoughts are triggered for you? Did you learn anything new about fertility in general or about what to anticipate if you have decided to pursue one of the options presented in this book? I truly hope so.

I did not imagine at any point in my life, or even during my fertility journey, that I would undergo so many experiences. As I reflect on the different chapters in this book, I am amazed at what I have lived through. And I know that I am not alone! I am also amazed that I mostly outlined and drafted this book while sitting in the hairdresser's chair when I found myself with free time. I am grateful I have been able to share all that I have learned about a variety of options for building a family, from IUI or IVF to adoption to gestational carriers and egg or sperm donors, in a more detailed and enduring way. I truly believe we can prevent what I went through with increased awareness in our field.

I know it will be uncommon for people to experience my journey; however, my journey, personally, has provided me with a unique perspective on a wide variety of nontraditional family planning pathways. Ultimately, I experienced the process of preparing for an adoption along with three IUIs, four egg retrievals, four rounds of IVF, and two embryo transfers with the assistance of a gestational carrier. While everyone likely will not need all these avenues, you may not know which is best for you, and I sincerely hope this guide helps you understand your options. I hope it also helps you anticipate ways to navigate a busy and demanding medical career while still pursuing fertility treatment if needed or desired.

For me, knowledge has always been power in this process. Even in the most powerless and hopeless of times, learning what options I had before me helped me move through grief and each stage towards my goal of becoming a parent.

I thought that perhaps some To-Do lists might be helpful for the reader, so they follow this chapter. This section can also serve as a bit of a fertility journal. You can log dates and thoughts for each phase of this journey.

Again, feel free to share your stories with me on Twitter @Jenna-MillerKC. You can also contact me or my GC via my website, jennamillermd. com, if you have questions or reflections on your journey.

I sincerely wish you luck in your endeavors!

To Do Lists

As I have experienced this journey, I kept notes on tasks required at each stage along the way. To follow this, there are several To Do lists associated with different chapters to help you keep track of tasks to complete. In the hard copy version of this guide, there are places to write dates and notes. Thus, this section may also serve as place to journal during your journey.

To Do-Chapter 4

Maintaining Preventative Health Care

☐ Consider ensuring you are up to date on vaccine preventable diseases.

Notes:

_____

_____

_____

☐ Ensure your annual Well-Woman Exam is up to date, including Pap, as recommended for your personal health history.

Date: _____

Notes:

_____

_____

_____

☐ For those over forty or with a history of high-risk breast cancer, update your annual mammogram.

Date: _____

Notes:

_____

_____

_____

To Do-Chapter 6

Where to Start-Fertility Treatments

☐ Review your health insurance.

Notes:

_____

_____

_____

☐ Research local ART clinics by talking with friends and coworkers and reading online reviews.

Notes:

_____

_____

_____

☐ Schedule a consultation appointment (ask about a cancellation waitlist).

Date_____

Notes:

_____

_____

_____

☐ Consider reading additional information about your intended process. (Refer to the resources in Ch. 5, *What Do All These Letters Mean?*)

Notes:

_____

_____

_____

To-Do: Chapter 7

Intrauterine Insemination (IUI)

☐ Select a Sperm Donor, if needed (See Ch. 11, *Egg Donors and Sperm Donors,* for more on this process).

Notes:

_____

_____

_____

☐ Schedule your cycle.

Start Date: _____

Notes:

_____

_____

_____

☐ Order your medications once prescribed by your clinic.

Notes:

_____

_____

_____

☐ Consider sharing with a trusted friend, family member, or coworker. Perhaps enlist the support of a therapist.

Notes:

_____

_____

_____

☐ Consider if any changes are required to accommodate the financial burden. Do you need to cut expenses? Or increase income?

Notes:

_____

_____

_____

☐ Consider your work schedule and check if you can be off the day of the IUI.

IUI Date Range: _____

Notes:

_____

_____

_____

To-Do: Chapter 8

Preparing for Egg Retrieval

☐ Select a Sperm Donor, if needed (See Ch. 11, *Egg Donors and Sperm Donors,* for more on this process).

Notes:

_____

_____

_____

☐ Schedule your cycle.

Start Date: _____

Notes:

_____

_____

_____

☐ Consider your work schedule and check if you can be off the day of retrieval and the day after.

Retrieval Date: _____

Notes:

_____

_____

_____

☐ Consider if acupuncture is something you want to begin.

Notes:

_____

_____

_____

☐ Begin recommended supplements, as applicable, and set daily reminders in your phone or planner.

Notes:

_____

_____

_____

☐ Consider sharing with a trusted friend, family member, or coworker. Perhaps enlist the support of a therapist.

Notes:

_____

_____

_____

☐ Consider if any changes are required to accommodate the financial burden. Do you need to cut expenses? Or increase income?

Notes:

_____

_____

_____

To-Do: Chapter 9

What to Expect during the Stimulation Phase

☐ Consider your work schedule and see if you can decrease or switch your clinical workload during the stimulation phase. Specifically, can you avoid night shifts?

Stimulation Start Date: _____

Retrieval Window Dates: _____

Notes:

_____

_____

_____

☐ Make your clinic appointments for monitoring.

Clinic Appointment Dates: _____

_____

_____

Notes:

_____

_____

_____

☐ Order your medications once prescribed by your clinic. You or a trusted
adult must be home to receive the medications.

Delivery Date: _____

Notes:

_____

_____

_____

☐ Read or view any materials given to you for your medications. Set daily
reminders to keep on schedule with injections.

Notes:

_____

_____

_____

Enlist someone to help you with your trigger shot, if desired.

Notes:

_____

_____

_____

To-Do: Chapter 10

What to Expect on Egg Retrieval Day and After

☐ Ensure you are off work during the retrieval window.

Retrieval Window Dates: _____

Notes:

_____

_____

_____

☐ Enlist a driver for your procedure day and ask someone to help you in your first twenty-four hours post-procedure.

Notes:

_____

_____

_____

☐ Follow up on how may mature eggs retrieved.

Number mature eggs: _____

Notes:

_____

_____

_____

☐ If you are proceeding with IVF, await the number of eggs that fertilized and then mature.

Number of eggs that fertilized:_____

Number of mature embryos: _____

Notes:

_____

_____

_____

☐ If in IVF, await the genetic results of mature embryos, as applicable.

Number of genetically healthy embryos: _____

Notes:

_____

_____

_____

To-Do: Chapter 11

Egg and Sperm Donors

Select an egg donor, if necessary

☐ Determine if you want a fresh or frozen cycle.

☐ Ask yourself the following questions if you find them valuable:

- *What kind of genetic screening has been done, and did that align with my personal carrier status?*

- *What blood types were compatible?*

- *How many children have been linked to this specific donor?*

- *Was the donor open to being contacted in the future by offspring?*

☐ Select a donor by screening available banks.

Notes:

_____

_____

_____

☐ Understand how many eggs you will receive in your cohort and whether there is a "blast guarantee." Place your order.

Notes:

_____

_____

_____

☐ Consider if any changes are required to accommodate the financial burden. Do you need to cut expenses? Or increase income?

Notes:

_____

_____

_____

Select a Sperm Donor, if necessary.

☐ Ask yourself the following questions if you find them valuable:

- *What kind of genetic screening has been done, and did that align with my personal carrier status?*

- *What blood types were compatible?*

- *How many children have been linked to this specific donor?*

- *Was the donor open to being contacted in the future by offspring?*

☐ Select a donor by screening available banks.

Notes:

_____

_____

_____

Understand how many vials you will need and place your order.

Notes:

_____

_____

_____

To-Do: Chapter 12

Gestational Carriers and Surrogates

☐ Determine if you will use a GC agency or if it will be someone you know.

Notes:

_____

_____

_____

☐ Monitor the results of GC health screening. Understand and anticipate the costs associated with this.

Notes:

_____

_____

_____

☐ Undergo a psychological evaluation as required by your clinic.

Notes:

_____

_____

_____

☐ Engage a lawyer for the contract negotiations.

Notes:

_____

_____

_____

☐ Consider having additional insurance coverage for your GC.

Notes:

_____

_____

_____

☐ Consider full-estate planning if it is not already done.

Notes:

_____

_____

_____

☐ Plan your GC transfer cycle dates.

Medication start date: _____

Transfer date: _____

Beta test day: _____

Notes:

_____

_____

_____

☐ Order medications for your GC when clinic has prescribed their order.

Notes:

_____

_____

_____

To-Do: Chapter 13

Embryo Transfer

☐ Plan for your transfer day. Will you be there for your GC, if applicable?
Do you need to take off from work?

Transfer date: _____

Notes:

_____

_____

_____

☐ If you have a GC or surrogate, are there any transportation arrangements
that need to be made? Do you want to bring a transfer day gift for her?

Notes:

_____

_____

_____

To-Do: Chapter 14

What about Adoption?

☐ Identify a list of agencies to research. This can be from a friend or family or coworker referral, searching your own city, or undergoing a national search.

Notes:

_____

_____

_____

☐ Schedule interviews with various agencies.

Notes:

_____

_____

_____

☐ Financially plan for the adoption fees if you receive a match.

Notes:

_____

_____

_____

☐ Select an agency and sign a contract.

Agency: _____

Notes:

_____

_____

_____

☐ Home Study process. This may be done with your agency, or you may need a local agency as well if your signed agency is a national group.

Home study agency: (may be same) _____

Notes:

_____

_____

_____

☐ Profile

Company Used to Create Profile_____

Notes:

_____

_____

_____

☐ Self-reflection on what your ideal situation is.

Notes:

_____

_____

_____

References

1. Infertility | Reproductive Health | CDC. Published March 3, 2022. Accessed December 18, 2022. https://www.cdc.gov/reproductivehealth/infertility/index.htm

2. ART Success Rates | CDC. Published June 14, 2022. Accessed December 18, 2022. https://www.cdc.gov/art/artdata/index.html

3. IVF children shown to have a better quality of life as adults in new study: First study to explore prosocial development of adults conceived with assisted reproductive technology show positive results. ScienceDaily. Accessed December 19, 2022. https://www.sciencedaily.com/releases/2022/03/220323101314.htm

4. Stentz NC, Griffith KA, Perkins E, Jones RD, Jagsi R. Fertility and Childbearing Among American Female Physicians. *J Womens Health (Larchmt)*. 2016;25(10):1059-1065. doi:10.1089/jwh.2015.5638

5. Aghajanova L, Hoffman J, Mok-Lin E, Herndon CN. Obstetrics and Gynecology Residency and Fertility Needs: National Survey Results. *Reproductive Sciences*. 2017;24(3):428-434. doi:10.1177/1933719116657193

6. Martin CE, Hipp HS, Kottke M, Haddad LB, Kawwass JF. Fertility, Pregnancy, and Postpartum: A Survey of Practicing Georgia Obstetrician Gynecologists. *Matern Child Health J*. 2019;23(10):1299-1307. doi:10.1007/s10995-019-02801-9

7. Rangel EL, Castillo-Angeles M, Easter SR, et al. Incidence of Infertility and Pregnancy Complications in US Female Surgeons. *JAMA Surg*. 2021;156(10):905. doi:10.1001/jamasurg.2021.3301

8. 2022 FACTS: Applicants and Matriculants Data. AAMC. Accessed December 30, 2022. https://www.aamc.org/data-reports/students-residents/interactive-data/2022-facts-applicants-and-matriculants-data

9. 2022 Report on Residents Executive Summary. AAMC. Accessed December 18, 2022. https://www.aamc.org/data-reports/students-residents/data/report-residents/2022/executive-summary

10. Young A, Chaudhry HJ, Pei X, Arnhart K, Dugan M, Simons KB. FSMB Census of Licensed Physicians in the United States, 2020. Published online 2021

11. Having a Baby After Age 35: How Aging Affects Fertility and Pregnancy. Accessed December 18, 2022. https://www.acog.org/en/womens-health/faqs/having-a-baby-after-age-35-how-aging-affects-fertility-and-pregnancy

12. Risch N, Stein Z, Kline J, Warburton D. The relationship between maternal age and chromosome size in autosomal trisomy. *Am J Hum Genet*. 1986;39(1):68-78.

13. Trends in Fertility and Mother's Age at First Birth Among Rural and Metropolitan Counties: United States, 2007-2017. Published June 7, 2019. Accessed December 18, 2022. https://www.cdc.gov/nchs/products/databriefs/db323.htm

14. National Summary Report. Society for Assisted Reproductive Technology. Accessed December 20, 2022. https://www.sartcorsonline.com/rptCSR_PublicMultYear.aspx

15. IVF Success Estimator | Assisted Reproductive Technology (ART) | Reproductive Health | CDC. Published August 4, 2021. Accessed December 18, 2022. https://www.cdc.gov/art/ivf-success-estimator/

16. Third Party Reproduction. Society for Assisted Reproductive Technology. Accessed December 18, 2022. https://www.sart.org/patients/third-party-reproduction/

17. Insurance Coverage by State | RESOLVE: The National Infertility Association. Published August 27, 2021. Accessed December 18, 2022. https://resolve.org/learn/financial-resources-for-family-building/insurance-coverage/insurance-coverage-by-state/

18. IUI Side Effects & Treatment: What to Expect? Apollo Fertility. Published July 26, 2019. Accessed December 18, 2022. https://www.apollofertility.com/blog/iui/iui-treatment-what-to-expect/

19. Rossi BV, Berry KF, Hornstein MD, Cramer DW, Ehrlich S, Missmer SA. Effect of alcohol consumption on in vitro fertilization. *Obstet Gynecol*. 2011;117(1):136-142. doi:10.1097/AOG.0b013e31820090e1

20. Hatch EE, Wesselink AK, Hahn KA, et al. Intake of Sugar-sweetened Beverages and Fecundability in a North American Preconception Cohort. *Epidemiology*. 2018;29(3):369-378. doi:10.1097/ EDE.0000000000000812

21. Hullender Rubin LE, Opsahl MS, Wiemer KE, Mist SD, Caughey AB. Impact of whole systems traditional Chinese medicine on in-vitro fertilization outcomes. *Reprod Biomed Online*. 2015;30(6):602-612. doi:10.1016/j.rbmo.2015.02.005

22. Rubin LH, DAOM, LAc, Medicine FA at OR, Studio PA. How Acupuncture Impacts IVF Success Rates. FertilityIQ. Accessed December 18, 2022. https://www.fertilityiq.com/topics/ acupuncture-for-fertility/how-acupuncture-impacts-ivf-success-rates

23. Katz-Jaffe MG, Lane SL, Parks JC, McCallie BR, Makloski R, Schoolcraft WB. Antioxidant Intervention Attenuates Aging-Related Changes in the Murine Ovary and Oocyte. *Life (Basel)*. 2020;10(11):250. doi:10.3390/life10110250

24. Tamura H, Nakamura Y, Korkmaz A, et al. Melatonin and the ovary: physiological and pathophysiological implications. *Fertil Steril*. 2009;92(1):328-343. doi:10.1016/j.fertnstert.2008.05.016

25. Gleicher N, Barad DH. Dehydroepiandrosterone (DHEA) supplementation in diminished ovarian reserve (DOR). *Reprod Biol Endocrinol*. 2011;9:67. doi:10.1186/1477-7827-9-67

26. Ben-Meir A, Burstein E, Borrego-Alvarez A, et al. Coenzyme Q10 restores oocyte mitochondrial function and fertility during reproductive aging. *Aging Cell*. 2015;14(5):887-895. doi:10.1111/ acel.12368

27. Hoang K, Evans N, Aghajanova L, Talib H, Linos E, Gold JM. Fertility Benefits at Top U.S. Medical Schools. *J Womens Health (Larchmt).* 2022;31(9):1369-1373. doi:10.1089/jwh.2021.0486

28. Ovarian Hyperstimulation Syndrome. Society for Assisted Reproductive Technology. Accessed December 18, 2022. https://www.sart.org/patients/a-patients-guide-to-assisted-reproductive-technology/stimulation/ovarian-hyperstimulation-syndrome/

29. Blastocyst. Mayo Clinic. Accessed December 29, 2022. https://www.mayoclinic.org/tests-procedures/in-vitro-fertilization/multimedia/blastocyst/img-20008646